Gestures

Other books by Roger E. Axtell:

Do's & Taboos Around the World, 2nd Edition, Wiley

The Do's & Taboos of International Trade: A Small Business Primer,
   Wiley

Do's & Taboos of Hosting International Visitors, Wiley

Gestures
The Do's and Taboos of
Body Language Around the World

Roger E. Axtell

Illustrated by Mike Fornwald

John Wiley & Sons, Inc.
New York • Chichester • Brisbane • Toronto • Singapore

Library of Congress Cataloging-in-Publication Data

Axtell, Roger E.
    Gestures: the do's and taboos of body language around the world /
by Roger E. Axtell.
        p.   cm.
    Includes index.
    ISBN 0-471-53672-5
    1. Gesture—Cross-cultural studies.   2. Nonverbal communication
(Psychology)—Cross-cultural studies.   3. Nonverbal communication—
Cross-cultural studies.   I. Title.
BF637.N66A88   1991
153.6'9—dc20   91-8001

Printed in the United States of America

10 9 8 7 6 5

Printed and bound by the Courier Companies, Inc.